WE BE BLACK, WE'VE BEEN BLUE

A black woman's perspective on being black and overcoming past blues

Rafequa C. Hall

ISBN: 979-8-9878817-0-5

We Be Black, We've Been Blue

Proudly self-published through Divine Legacy Publishing, www.divinelegacypublishing.com

Book Cover: Rose Miller
Cover Illustrator: Cosmin Constantin Crucean
Illustrations: Alanna C. Hall
Author Photo: Ashleigh Carby
Author Makeup: Kirston's Kit

WHAT HAPPENS WHEN THE
NEXT GENERATION
SEARCHES NOT FOR THE TRUTH
AND SETTLES TO DRINK FROM
THE BITTER FOUNTAIN OF
RACE COMPLACENCY?

-RAFEQUA C. HALL

POEMS

PART ONE – BLACK, YES WE BE THAT
Cultural

PART TWO – THESE BLUES BE BURDENSOME
Life
Self-Awareness
Relationship
Abuse

Rafequa C. Hall

PART ONE

Black, yes we be that

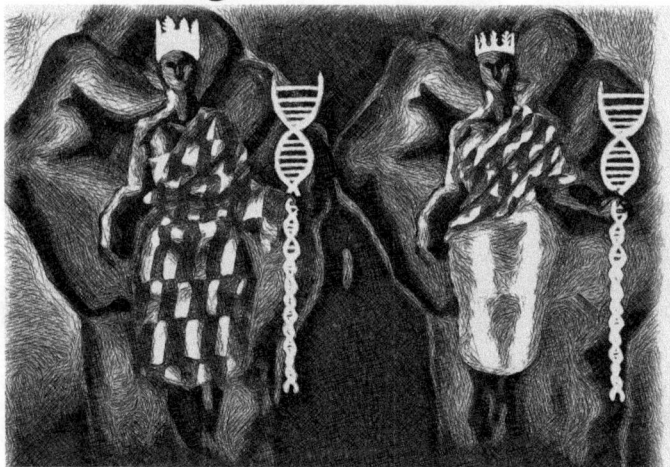

CULTURAL

SURE, MUST BE SOMETHING

PREFACE:
History class spoke of slavery. We knew about black oppression, injustices, and dehumanization. We spoke about blacks being treated to feel as if they were an inferior race.
Before the Trans-Atlantic slave trade, we were.
We were more than we were told.

TONE:
Educational, Strong, Empowering

Mentally
Emaciated

Our souls
Salivating.

Groaning with hunger
Like unsettling sounds of thunder.

Starved,
Famished for the truth.

I ask you,
Have you ever wondered?

Rafequa C. Hall

Have you ever
Forced your mind

To question your soul?

Interrogate the stories
You were told?

Open your eyes.
Can't you see?
They are feeding you lies.

I ask you
Why?
Why is there so much hate?

Hate for our race…

Don't take the bait.
His tactics
Are to erase us,

Disgrace us,

Manipulate and rape us.

We are the targeted race
It's such a disgrace.

Hmm…blacks sure, must be something,
Even though we're treated like nothing.

Is it our strength?
Is it our soul?

We Be Black, We've Been Blue

Is it the cost of the melanin tone?
Is it their fear of the anger in our eyes?
Is it the fact that we are
Prized?
Prized with a calling from the beginning of time?
Is it knowing the truth
Of the power
We hold inside?

Denied the right to read,
Yet we were smart
In secret we'd teach each
Other how to succeed.

Break every chain to overcome,
Through trials and tribulations
We shall overcome!

With your weights
On our backs
Still we rise,
Education should not be deprived
We deserve quality lives.

Huh! Blacks sure must be something
Even though we're treated like nothing.

I can't keep from thinking
How we are muffled from speaking!
Plagued by the past
Similar to Sandra Bland
Hands up, shut up
Like back in slavery.

Rafequa C. Hall

Ain't nothing change
This ain't new
Come on y'all, this is obvious
And it's true.

Erased your past,
Replaced your name,
Stole your land.
Sold your ancestors
Putting asunder
What God has joined together.

Separating and more separation
Much like abortion, suction
Ripped right out the womb
Integration whom?
Tearing the child straight from the womb.
Innocent yet the blood was shed

Echoes of screams beyond the grave
Echoes of screams from captured slaves
Echoes of screams we protest!
Echoes of screams for injustice!

Screaming for years
These tears are ancient
Screaming for years
We've run out of patience
Screaming for years
Our voice we didn't lose

Begging and pleading
To loosen the noose
Begging and pleading

Please don't shoot
Begging and pleading
For our lives…

WHY are we begging pleading
For human rights?

Who are we?

Have you ever asked?

You are damn sure something
Even though they treat you like nothing
We are more than we were told
Kings and Queens from majestic thrones

Erased your past
Replaced your name
Stole your land
Sold your ancestors
Attempting to destroy your soul

Soulfully soul
Humming that tune
It's a strange thing,
It's a strange fruit
To me it was
More like a rotten fruit
Rotten for generations
Planting their seeds
To destroy our black nation

They would frame you,
Muzzle you, like a dog

Rafequa C. Hall

You better not sing that song.

We peer through windows of the past
Pulling back the shade with disgust
Clear as the day meets the sun
Yesterday is much like today
Muffled mouths with much to say

Birds sing freely
Why can't we?

If speaking the truth is freedom
Why aren't we free yet?

Huh blacks sure must be something
Even though were treated like nothing

Black is almost like a type of Christ
The similarities we hold inside
Persecution and hate he beard
They feared him and jeered him
But he knew the power he held inside

He sure was something even though
They treated him like nothing

Relentless he was to the grave
We pray that God
Give us the same measure of grace
Help us to endure to the end
This I'll tell you my friend

It is our strength
It is our soul

It is the cost of the melanin tone
It is their fear of the anger in our eyes
It is the fact that we are
Prized
Prized with a calling
From the beginning of time
Knowing the truth of the power
That we hold inside

Our rightful position could never be sold
It is the fact that
We are more
Than we were told
Yes,
We are Kings and Queens from majestic thrones.

Rafequa C. Hall

A people without the knowledge of their history, origin and culture is like a tree without roots.

- Marcus Garvey

It is that which constitutes our real and best nourishment. What we are merely taught seldom nourishes the mind like that which we teach ourselves.

-Carter G. Woodson
The Mis-Education of The Negro

African Kingdoms/Empires

1. Almohad Empire
2. Kingdom of Kush
3. The Benin Empire
4. Ashanti Empire
5. The Aksum Kingdom
6. The Zulu Kingdom
7. The Kingdom of Kongo
8. The Kingdom of Ghana
9. The Kingdom of Dagbon
10. Mali Empire
11. Songhai Empire
12. The people of Kemet

Kings/Emperors/Pharaohs

1. King Mansa Musa - Mali Empire
2. King Sunni Ali Bear - 1st king of the Songhai Empire
3. King Endubis of the great kingdom of Aksum
4. Oba Ewuare- Benin's Browne king
5. King Shaka Zulu- Zulu Kingdom
6. King Yusuf Abir Tashfin
7. King Zoser
8. King Menkaure
9. Pharaoh ThutmoseIII
10. Pharaoh AmenhotepIII
11. Pharaoh Taharqa
12. Pharaoh Khufu
13. Emperor Menelik II
14. King Idris Alooma- King of the Kanem-Bornu empire

Queens

1. Queen Ndate Nyalla
2. Queen Mwana Mikisi
3. Queen Nandi-Zulu Kingdom South Africa
4. Queen Amina-of Zaria Nigeria
5. Warrior Queen Makeda-The queen of Sheba, Ethiopia
6. Quneen Idia
7. Empress Taitu
8. Empress Kandake of Ethiopia
9. Warrior Queen Nzingha
10. Queen of Kemet- Hatshepsut
11. Queen Nzinga
12. Queen Moremi from the Yoruba kingdom
13. Nubian Queen Amanitore
14. Queen Nanny of the Maroons

*The above is <u>not</u> an exhaustive list but only a few are listed above.

**Yes, there were slaves in Africa and other parts of the world and other times in history. Nothing compared to the mistreatment and injustice of the transatlantic slave trade.

HARMONY NEVER HAD A HOME

SETTING:
The Civil War ends and the 13th amendment to the
U.S. Constitution abolishes slavery in the south, Jim
Crow laws begin.

PREFACE:
Despite them not being slaves anymore and now pro-
claimed free, there was still no harmony but hate that
continued to reside.

TONE:
Solemn

The whipping, whistling winds
Rustled through the southern willow trees.
Never whispered a word
Nor wondered

Where is harmony?

Harmony never had a home
No, not here.

No, not anywhere.
No, not by
The muddy banks of the lower Mississippi River,
Where the depths of history dug its liquid graves,
Where the current flowed to free some slaves.

Harmony never had a home
No, not here.
No, not anywhere

Not by the
Timeless trickling trails of tears
That taunted far too many

Harmony never played a single note
Not by the
Plantation fields,
Where they deeply planted seeds of hate
While picking cotton near the cemetery,
Where the dead bodies of the enraged lay.

Harmony had no home in the southern streets
Or way out yonder

The absence of her presence
Ignited spirits with unpleasant fumes of gasoline
While torching a fire deep within the tanks of our
hearts
Voices cried out with a fierce venomous vengeance
Moans and groans of anguish and agony from the ab-
sence of harmony
Tears, fears, tiredness, and frustration.

Testing our faith and challenging our patience.
Humanity was so off key
Singing a tune with no harmony

No sonnets
No symphonies
Not a single melody

We Be Black, We've Been Blue

And surely no harmony

Dreadfully divided devalued dark discordance resided
Hostility
Clashing
Clambering
Cymbals
Loud obnoxious
Symbols
Showing nothing but hate
Swaying
Confederate flags.

Harmony never had a home
Even the birds sang off key
Lacking the sweet melody of unity
As the soulless, songless sounds of
Vultures grunting
Hissing the devil's tune of Ol' Jim Crow

Our people were humming the blues while drumming
To the beat of millions of shoes
Weary souls,
Soles walking where they used to run
Passing dead bodies of their families hung
Wading in the waters
While waiting to hear if the freedom bell had rung

Let the trumpets trump.
The emancipation proclamation had come,
Exclaiming that slavery is done.

This is the tune the trumpet had
Trumped.

Racism resides amongst us,
Injustice inhabits our court systems,
Economic inequality lives within our institutions.

Yet harmony is still homeless

Still
Less

And less

If there be less of anything

Let there be

Less blue on black
Less black on black
Less white vs black
Less holding each other back

Still

Stands time

Time stands

Watching as we let it slip
Idly by
Waiting as we
Waste precious time
Hoping one day we can get it right

Imprinting our fingers

On these bricks that builds
A better tomorrow
Engraved with the words
Harmony lived here!

Music is an expression of harmony in sound. Love is an expression of harmony in life.

- Stephen Gaskins

It takes black keys and white keys to make perfect Harmony.

-Benny Goodman

We be BLACK &
We've been BLUE

SETTING:
It took place in May of 1921, in the Greenwood district of Tulsa, Oklahoma.
A place where economic growth and prosperity resided. A black community came to a burning and deadly destructive halt, consuming dreams and life. Through the strength and solidarity of some survivors and alliances, Greenwood was rebuilt.
*Please also note this wasn't the only black Wall Street or thriving wealthy black community that existed in history; this was the only one that ended in a massacre.

PREFACE:
Description and imagining the experience of the Tulsa Massacre.

TONE:
Solemn, educational, empowering

Hold your breath

Or you will choke

From the truth
Never taught
But told to me
From TV

Rafequa C. Hall

1921
Death dared to dance
On thousands
Of ancestral dreams

Damnation
Documented
As history,

History
Holds hell in
His hands while
Tormenting Tulsa

Tightening
His hellish grip

Hear the fear
Through the air
Crackling flames
Bombs blasting

Burning
Black businesses
And homes
Putrid stench of
Deathly decaying
Black burnt bodies

Sudden silence
For decades
They dared
Not speak
Their tongues tied

To graves
Unable to utter or mutter
A single word
Terrified,
Some mentally paralyzed

Send a sudden
Thundering
Shout from heaven
Speak, oh God to our people.

Tell them to be
Triumphant in the day of terror.

Tell them at once
To be awaken

Tell them to
Command courage to come quickly

Tell them to
Escape the entrapment and encourage their hearts

Tell them to
Lift their lowly sunken spirits

Show these shadows
Of shame the strength
We hold
In the belly of this here beast

STAND

Stand strong

Rafequa C. Hall

Stand tall

STAND

Lift your spirits from dust

STAND

Hold your head high
Sing such spirituals

Walk through the fire
Sing such spirituals

Through the flames with grace
Sing such spirituals

Search yourself, find again
Yourself
Self-respect
Self-reliance
Self-esteem
Say to Self
I will be!

God granted fuel of faith
Fainted they did not!

Souls stood up with such a mighty force
Strived with strivings
Greater than a million-foot wave
Arise and yet survive

Rise

We Be Black, We've Been Blue

Dare to stare fear in its face.
They said in this land we will stay.

The will to rebuild

Rebuild,
They did
In this here
Unrighteousness

Amongst the smoldering remnants
Resilience resuscitated
From the hellish
Heap of decaying death

The winds of time blew on by
Erasing the footprints found faded in the ashes

The lesson is a legacy lent to sisters and brothers
Born black yet lived blue
Generationally
Past, present and currently you
Me
Him
Her
They
Them
Our children
Grandchildren and
Great grands

Children
Come

Rafequa C. Hall

There's work to be done
Waste not want not
No place for complacency
Leave your family a legacy

Let us be

We be black!
We be no more blue!

We be wealth!
We be each economically empowered!
We be bold!
We be more than gold!

Black!
Yes, we be that!

We be proud!
We say it loud!

Face your focus not on anger
Focus forward facing the future
Forget not where we've come from
Know the truth
Not HIS-story but
OURS
For therein lies the power!

We Be Black, We've Been Blue

There is but one coward on earth, and that is the
coward that dare not know.

— W.E.B. DuBois
Dusk of Dawn

- 108 Black owned businesses
- 41 Grocery and meat markets
- 35 City blocks
- 21 Churches
- 30 Restaurants
- 2 News papers
- 9 Billiards halls
- Hotels
- Night clubs
- 2 Movie theaters
- 6 Private planes
- A hospital
- A bank
- Beauty Salons & Barbers
- A post office
- Schools
- Libraries
- Law offices
- A bus system
- Physicians and surgeons
- Real Estate and insurance agents
- Lawyers
- Greenwood avenue
- May 30th - June 1st of 1921
- Memorial Day
- 18 Hours of destruction
- Black history's heart bleeds blue
- Booker T. Washington named it Black Wall Street
- O.W. Hurley-purchased 40 acres of land

- Hurley founded Vernon AME Church
- Economic empowerment entrepreneur
- Home to 10k black residents
- Wealthiest black community in US

Rebuilding

- "The speed at which residents began to rebuild their neighborhood is astonishing, especially considering that within a week of the near-total destruction of Greenwood"
- "It wasn't just homes that were rebuilt. The businesses came back, too."
- "They just were not going to be kept down. They were determined not to give up," recalled Eunice Jackson, a survivor of the massacre, in an interview for Eddie Faye Gates' 1997 book, They Came Searching. "So they rebuilt Greenwood and it was just wonderful. It became known as The Black Wall Street of America." https://www.smithsonianmag.com/history/black-wall-streets-second-destruction-180977871/

Other Black Wall Streets

- "But Tulsa's was not the only Black Wall Street. The history of other such districts nationwide is still not widely known beyond their home cities, though they were many: Bronzeville in Chicago; Hayti in Durham, N.C.; Sweet Auburn in Atlanta; West Ninth Street in Little Rock, Ark.;

and Farish Street in Jackson, Miss."
https://time.com/6050811/tulsa-black-wall-street/

Author's Insight:

Life is not meant for us to become comfortable and complacent in our past, present, or current state.

We should always be in a state of growing, learning, and always striving for better.

Settling is never an option; be your best, do your best and give your best, then repeat.

Even during the toughest moments in life, you have the opportunity to focus forward, and push past the pain.

Moments may come when you feel stuck and feel the need to give up. Giving up will get you nowhere fast, so it should never be an option. Challenge yourself to do something different- you just may get a better result.

Listen - it takes no effort to do nothing. Before you know it, years may pass and you will be stuck in the same mess, repeating the same lessons.

Sometimes the hardest battles are won, when we accept the uncomfortable truths and learn how to move out of your state of comfort, no matter how difficult it may seem.

COMPLACENCY

PREFACE:
The negative impact of complacency in one's life.

TONE:
Serious and Critical

Call complacency a killer,
A low down and dirty deceiver
Cold and calculated,
A cancerous growth.

Canceling dreams
Tucking you subtly, comfortably
Like rotten meat tucked tightly
between decaying teeth.

The tragedy of life is not found in failure but complacency. Not in you doing too much, but doing too little. Not in you living above your means, but below your capacity. It's not failure but aiming too low, that is life's greatest tragedy.

-Benjamin E. Mays

Rafequa C. Hall

MUD PIES AND WORN SHOES

PREFACE:
How a young black girl back in the days destroyed her blues.

TONE:
Nostalgic, reminiscent

Little black girl
Buried her blues in mud pies
And baked them in sunshine

She'd run those blues loose
Playing in her worn-out shoes

> Red light/Green light
> Screaming 1, 2, 3 Not IT!
> Mother may I
> Dodgeball
> Kick ball
> Hide & Seek
> T.V. Tag
> You name it we played it
> Hot peas and butter, come and
> get your super
> Jumping rope
> Double Dutch
> Hopscotch

Singing "All, all, all in together
now"

Back in the days
We used to play
Black girl
Hand games like

Slide baby
Rockin Robin
Shame, shame, shame
Punchanella
Down by the bank of the hanky
panky
Miss Mary Mack
Down Down Baby

Latchkey kids
Placed shoelaces through keyholes
Then placed it around their neck.

You know the code
Don't tell a soul your home alone.
Promises pinned to punishment
Found in my mother's eyes
Piercingly she stares straight through me,
I could never lie.

I'd rather just die
Than not go outside
And run my blues loose
Playin' in my worn-out shoes.

Punishment that would last for years

I'd cry a monsoon if I broke her rules.

My mother held down two and three jobs.
Tootsie toughed it through
Hustling three to eleven-
Matter of fact, 24/7.

Friends became sitters
Sitters suddenly shapeshifted into families
Families that turned blues into built bridges.

Bridging the gap, building the biggest monuments of
memories
Like angels, sent to turn our blues into beauty.
Like mama, Grandma Jewel, Grandma Johnson, The
Johnson Family, uncles and aunties.
It was a duty
It took a village, y'all.

Some days or on Sundays she'd share
Sardines and rice for dinner.

On Saturdays she'd cook her Jamaican chicken foot
soup

Other days I'd chug a glass of
Sharkoberry Kool Aid
After a long school day.

Mom held it down and for that she should be proud.

You'd think every day was blue, but we did what we
had to do.

My mother made do. Our friends and our neighbors
did too.

Life was bad yet life was good.
The 80's and 90's growing up was tough,
Yet we had days with so much fun, playing in the sum-
mer's sun.

This little black girl
Buried her blues in mud pies
And baked them in sunshine

I'd run my blues loose
Playing in my worn-out shoes.

Rafequa C. Hall

We are our own healing place.

- Melvina Young

SISTA

PREFACE:
"Sista"
This is indeed a terminology that is used so loosely
when two women of color meet.

TONE:
Bothered, Uplifting

Sista
Bitter as lemon lime.
Piercingly staring
Straight through me
Side eyein'
Fake smilin'

But you continue to call me SISTA

They say
Blood is thicker than water
And if that is the case
Then
We ain't blood
We're more like
Trickling water

Not quite like
Ebony and Ivory
Unfortunately,
We never lived in perfect harmony

Rafequa C. Hall

Yet, you call me SISTA

Same race
Same gender
Different agendas
Deceptive heart
Despising what you lack,
So you take and take

Toxic as gas
Seeping through your pores
Your intentions are never pure
Miscalculated,
Envious
Pretentious
For sure.
Like a fire-breathing dragon
Spewing sarcastic fumes

I contacted poison control
They instructed me to
STAY FAR AWAY FROM YOU!

Utilizing every lying adjective
Is your plan to derail another.
Then you paint a picture
And name it

SISTA?

Please do not call me
Your sista
I'd rather you call me by my name

We Be Black, We've Been Blue

Sayin' sis
Well, that would signify
Mutual respect

You dig?

You dig what you dug
Your actions were my lessons
The lesson was learned
Now school is done!

To you I ceased to speak
Employing the hearts and minds of others
Recruiting them to turn against me
Like sheep easily done
Takes no convincing
And so you feel the battle
Has been won.

We from the
Same race
Same tribe
Your family is mine
But you blatantly disregarded
The pain in my eyes
Used it as an opportunity for you to rise
God saw from heaven
And gave me wings to fly

For you what was harvested you must now retrieve
from fields of thorns...OUCH!

The term
Sista- ain't no trend

Rafequa C. Hall

In my book or any book

SISTERHOOD
Has its roots embedded deep
In the richest black soil
Fertilized by our past
Sistas of old
Sistas of soul

Sistas whose lives
Blessed us with beautiful poems
May Miller
Maya Angelou
Marita Bonner
Margaret Danner
Margaret Walker

Penning the past poetically
Presently them we praise
Whether Renaissance
Or post Renaissance
Their past paved the way

Sistas stepping with melodic symphonic chants,
Clapping hands
Stomping rhythmic feet,
Formations of
Synchronized bodies
Whether it be
AKA's or Delta Sigma Theta
We can't forget the Zeta's

Sistahood

We Be Black, We've Been Blue

Never made me feel misunderstood
Uplifting words and deeds;
Where unity and loyalty
Never cease to be

It's beautiful
It's healing
Empowering
And uplifting

S-
Me and my sis
So soulfully intertwined,
Never intimidated by each other's beauty, talent, or
smile.

I-
Intermingling our intelligent minds,
Meddling into conversation that leads to elevation.

S-
Shout out to you sis,
For sticking through the hard times.

T-
Tellin' me about myself,
When I'm wrong and when I'm right.

A-
Always having my back
As I have yours,
Cheerleaders for one another
Sista trips, if we shopping we sharing,
Never staring each other down

Rafequa C. Hall

You're my sista
I need ya to make it,
You bring the best of me out!

True sistas are more than sistas,
We are each other's
Sista,
Mother,
Friend
With whom I'd ride with until the very end!

She is a friend of mine. She gathers me, man. The pieces I am, she gathers them and gives them back to me in all the right order.

- Toni Morrison

Abandon the cultural myth that all female friendships must be bitchy, toxic or competitive. This myth is like heels and purses- pretty but designed to slow women down.

-Roxane Gay

A friend is one who knows us, but loves us anyway.

-Jerome Cummings

Si-sta: noun
The best kind of friend
Sistamotherfriend: A friend that is more than a friend.

-Rafequa C. Hall

PART TWO

These blues be burdensome

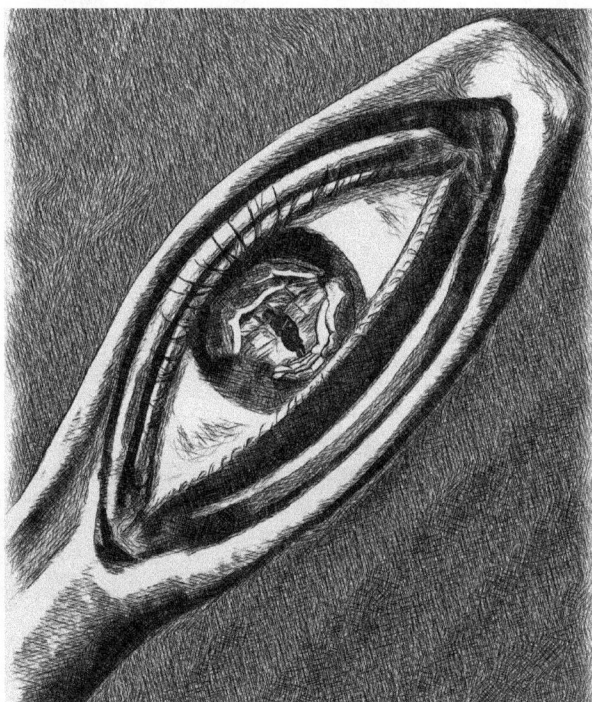

LIFE

Author's Insight:

I found the best parts of me during the worst times of life.

It was the moments I was made to be alone within myself, laying lifeless not on the sandy seashore of life but on the seafloor.

Heavy-hearted, soul -sunken below the deep blue sea, sinking suddenly. I was without air, stricken with fear drowning downwardly spiraling out of control in my troubles.

Instead of fighting through the tough times, I learned to just float in it. I learned to sit patiently in rough waters, wait in it, hold it, accept it.

Suddenly, I was able to pray through it and when I had no words to pray, I would praise through it. Then I grew to hear the instructions that guided me through, which taught me the art of silencing your mind through meditation.

I was exactly where I needed to be: raw and real.

Life dealt the cards and there was no reneging. I was forced to face myself as well as my thoughts.

Refusing to numb any part of it, refusing to hide from the truth. Refusing to give up or give in. I dug deep within me and oh I got to know all I needed.

I learned control, focus, peace, strength. The things the world or people can't give you, the things money can't buy but are highly valued. The things that are necessary for personal growth, and to gain strength.

Hardships help you to harness the power deep within yourself to overcome life toughest challenges and elevate you to the next level.

There was a time when I can honestly say I didn't know myself. I can't say that today…I'm so glad.

Rafequa C. Hall

THROUGH A NEEDLE'S EYE

PREFACE:
Keep God your focus when you are going through the
tough and weighty times in life. Give no ear to what
you hear, what they say or what you see. Place not your
eyes on what's around you, focus not on what they do.
God will lead you and guide you and see you through.
He will instruct you, and although at times you may
seem alone. He will never leave you nor forsake you.

TONE:
Encouraging, Spiritual, Insightful

On my way home
I sat in a packed subway car,
Gazing at an older woman who sat nearby.
Zoned into what she was doing,
She never lifted her eyes.
Unaffected by the stench of urine
And burnt brake pads.
She remained focused,
And steadfast,
Unbothered by the conductor
Yelling for each stop.
Unbothered by the loud music blaring
And cussing
As the train car rocked.
She kept her focus

Despite the obscene atmosphere.

Sitting sanctimoniously, stitching the garment of her life
While many sat near.
She didn't care,
Never mind who stopped,
Who laughed,
Who mocked or stared.

I looked at her face
And her eyes told a story;
Almost as if her life began to unfold
Right before me.
From the look in her eyes,
You could tell she had experienced life.
With a content look on her face
She took that needle and began stitching.

She wove worn and torn materials of her life.
Lugging these materials over her back
For quite some time
A luggage loaded with heavy burdens
The pressure
Weighed her down,
The hardship of life is what I glimpsed in her eyes.

Pulling her burdens through the eye of the needle
What a struggle, what a fight.
Diligently she sat patiently with her legs crossed,
Humming the tune to a spiritual song as if she knew the
tough times would not last long.

Battered, bruised, used, misused, confused,
She continued to stitch.

I guess she felt that they could be reused.

Through the needle's eye, she regained her life.
I asked her how she did it
She replied.
"One stitch at a time."

I said, "How did you sit through it with such a smile?"
"You couldn't see," she said.
"God sat by my side, and stayed with me at all times."
"You couldn't hear," she said
"As he whispered in my ear:
"*My child, have no fear,*
I will not put more on you than you can bear."

So do not fear, for I am with you; do not be dis-
mayed, for I am your God. I will strengthen you
and help you; I will uphold you with my righteous
right hand.

-Isaiah 41:10

The Lord is my strength and my song; he has
given me victory.

-Exodus 15:2

Rafequa C. Hall

GOLDEN FINCHES

PREFACE:
In every dark moment, God is always the light.

TONE:
Reminiscent, Hopeful, Spiritual

Man, goldfinches how pretty are they,
Never eva
Have I ever
Noticed them, until this one day.
When my world turned grey.

As I walked up a hill on Chester pike
No one could feel or hear
The heaviness of my sighs.
This hill I climbed was so steep
I could feel the burn in my thighs...
But still I pressed on
I continued to climb.

The rain began to drop
Hitting my face
Making it so easy to disguise the pain.

See each tear that dropped
Flowed
It blended
With the tears
That dropped from the sky

It's almost as if God cried
Cried with me,
Cried for me.

I spoke to him every step of the way.
Refusing to give way
To the negative thoughts.
Instead, I encouraged myself to just hold on.

I strived
Because I knew I was almost home.
I just pressed on to my refuge,
My humble abode.
You see, my daddy is always home.

So, I knock, knock, knock.
"Daddy, it's me.
Seems like this pain
Don't wanna leave!
This issue in my life
Won't seem to cease.
So, I come to you, God Almighty!"
I thought… maybe we could meet
Meet as I walk
Walk as I talk
Talk to you,
You are my relief.
You relieve my every pain
Stay with me every step, I pray
I need you in the most desperate way."

Man goldfinches how pretty are they

Never eva have I ever noticed them

Except for this one day.

Like I said the rain was falling… I had no umbrella
I didn't even care,
All that mattered was that my father was right there.

The rain fell hard, and my heart sank low.
Darkness filled the sky
To my great surprise two gold, black, and white birds
Flew right by.

A smile greeted my face
I knew who they were from.

Frightened that I witnessed,
Something so beautiful as two goldfinches.
To cross my path to remind me those grey skies won't
last.
I just smiled seeing the humor in how you dried my
eyes
And brought such sweet joy to my life.

No one would believe me if I told them.
How iconic these birds have become to me.

Just to know
You see me,
How you treat me,
You meet me
Exactly where I am.
You fill every empty space that I have.

You amaze me,
You soothe me,

We Be Black, We've Been Blue

You brighten my day!
I'm amazed that you continually send me
Two goldfinches on my rainiest days!

Rafequa C. Hall

I love to think of nature as an unlimited broadcast-
ing station, through which God speaks to us every
hour, if we will only tune in.
                    -George Washington Carver

STATE OF MIND

PREFACE:
The mind is fragile. Mind your mind.

TONE:
Educational, Encouraging, and Informative

All that boggles the mind
Keeps it running like the speed of light.
One thing after the other
So many things in so little time.

I need somewhere to go and free my mind
There is nowhere to run, nowhere to hide.
In this world so full of strife
I just need somewhere to go and release my sighs.

Distress heavy on my chest
Like lifting ten tons
I'm pressed
Persistently
Pounding
Palpitating
I'm profusely perspiring
Panicking,
I'm paralyzed with paranoia
Hyperventilating,
Trying to catch my breath
Tingling in each one of my extremities
I'm dreading
This impending doom

Rafequa C. Hall

From nowhere came this sudden fear
So now I'm here
Thinking…

Carnally minded… Why are you so blinded?
The perils of life, keeps you side-tracked
How do you plan on escaping the pressures of life?

Blind in sight,
Deaf in hearing
How do you expect to know where you're headed?

All that boggles the mind
Keeps it running like the speed of light
One thing after the other
So many things
So little time.
I need somewhere to go and free my mind

God keeps it running
His word is my guide
In darkness he is my light
Pouring out my soul
He has total control
Releasing my tears
Exposing my fears
Lifting my faith
On my knees I escape
Inhale/exhale

One blessing after another, he is always right on time.
On my knees I freed my mind.
To him I go under his wings. I do abide.

Trust in God.
Live by His words.
Leave it up to Him and let Him decide
Because your fate determines you,
The darkness of others can overshadow you,
The hatred in their heart can consume you too.

As bad as it seems, there is always hope if you believe.
Believe in God and you will achieve strength,
Happiness and joy from within.

Rafequa C. Hall

You may not control all the events that happen to you, but you can decide not to be reduced by them.
- Maya Angelou

WHERE LOVE LIVES

PREFACE:
Longing for a better world.

TONE:
Thoughtful and contemplative

We hold hurt like bandages,
wrapped up ever so tightly
bracing broken bones.
Though we'd hoped for hurt to heal, that never hap-
pened.
We walk around with limps, wearing it as the latest
fashion.

Hurt has been trending before hieroglyphics on ancient
monuments.
Our mummies
nursed us while praying that their generational curses be
reversed.

Then they sent us to churches where we rehearsed,
church hurt concealed in hymns, hallelujahs
tucked ever so tightly in fancy hats that dared to distract
the disillusioned with discreetly decorated feathers.
May we learn to lead, lifting up holy love as a bright
light.

Let's start serving sacred communion from the plate
and cup of self-love.

Lord, let the language we learn not be taught from
those who so eloquently speak a love language derived
from hurt people who hurt people.

Where is the house that love lives?
Where are the investors that will invest in it?
Pending are the present petitions of parents hoping to
pour concrete promises, setting a sure foundation to se-
cure a better nation.

Where is this house that love lives?
I've rummaged through these states, if this house had
feet I'm sure it escaped from these United States.

Unapologetically I state
love does not abide in these 50 states.
Not here where the homeless live hopeless.
Where hunger hides in hollow cabinets.
Where mothers weep while wondering how to feed
their famished families.

Where the streets are bumper to bumper filled with
trafficking.
These streets are paved with the silent yet astonishing
statistics stating between 15,000 to 50,000 women and
children soullessly snatched and sentenced into sexual
slavery.

Who unlocked the gate to leave insecurities in each and
every state?

I'm sure the house where love lives grew feet and escaped.

Rafequa C. Hall

The country is in deep trouble. We've forgotten that a rich life consists fundamentally of serving others, trying to leave the world a little better than you found it. We need the courage to question the powers that be, the courage to be impatient with evil and patient with people, the courage to fight for social justice. In many instances we will be stepping out on nothing, and just hoping to land on something. But that's the struggle. To live is to wrestle with despair, yet never allow despair to have the last word.

- Cornel West

Never forget that justice is what love looks like in public.

- Cornel West

HOUR GLASS

PREFACE:
Enjoy each moment of life. Be intentionally present.

TONE:
Insightful, Encouraging

By the seashore of life, we stand
Digging our feet in the sand
Tightly holding
Each other's hands

Telling jokes,
Watching folks

We laugh
Taking photographs
While time rapidly pass

Insignificant as it may seem
In a moment it can cease to be

Enjoy each day,
What we do
What we say
Never knowing
If the next moment
Will be our
Last.

Rafequa C. Hall

Who knows where the time goes?
                              - Nina Simone

PSALMS 23

PREFACE:
Don't die in your valley. No matter how dark it seems
to follow the light, God is the light. Go within, seek sol-
itude, quiet your mind, encourage your heart, and just
hold on. He reveals, He illuminates, allows you to hear
and see what you ordinarily couldn't. God will guide
you while going through the valley.

TONE:
Encouraging

Suddenly
I'm sinking silently
Swallowed in sorrow, submerging in me.
Tired of trying to stay afloat,
Drowning in tears, I'm sinking
Without a boat.

On mountains
I've climbed a number of times.
I've seen high peaks, and spent quality time.
Though huge mountains and peaks
Now surround me

In the valley
Is where I seem to be.

In the valley
Darkness resides both night and day
In the valley

Rafequa C. Hall

It seems death and fear have come to stay.

In the valley
I felt alone and afraid.

In the valley
God said do not be dismayed.

In the valley
God gave me Psalms 23.

In the valley
God granted me perfect peace.

A Psalm of David

"The LORD is my shepherd; I shall not want.
He maketh me to lie down in green pastures:
He leadeth me beside the still waters.
He restoreth my soul:
He leadeth me in the paths of righteousness for his name's sake.
Yea, though I walk through the valley of the shadow of death, I will fear no evil:
for thou art with me; Thy rod and thy staff they comfort me.
Thou preparest a table before me in the presence of mine enemies:
Thou anointest my head with oil; my cup runneth over.
Surely goodness and mercy shall follow me all the days of my life:
And I will dwell in the house of the LORD forever."

-Psalms 23

Rafequa C. Hall

SUNSHOWERS

PREFACE:
Storms come suddenly when you least expect it. Learn to appreciate the storms of life. Sometimes the storms bring about the most beautiful promises.

TONE:
Encouraging

The sun was beaming,
Steaming
It was scorching hot
Like scotch bonnet seeds
The intense kiss of the heated rays
Penetrated, permeated her melanin
Leaving her coated in bronze.

The sun was glaring, gleaming
It was golden bright
Skin like brown sugar
Melting into a syrupy sweat.
Excessively trickling, tickling as
It
Ran
Down
Her
Neck.

      Still

There were no clouds

We Be Black, We've Been Blue

In sight.

Beautiful variations of blue hues
Filled the sky,
Who knew
Suddenly
Bursting bouts of
Whipping, whistling, winds
Would begin to
Wheel wildly like a whirlwind.

Then came the rain
Pour
    Pour
        Pour

        Pour down you
                Pouring torrential rain.

Ignoring the brightly shining sun
Yet never hindering the gleaming rays.

Oh rain
    Rain
        Rain
She thanked the Lord for the torrential rain
Even the sudden pain
That life
Passed her way

Flow
    Flow
        Flow

Rafequa C. Hall

You rapid river of tears
Filling her deep dark brown eyes
Overflowing from life's pain
Like rivers running
Deep.
Deeper than the big blue sea.

You see
Sun showers

Release
Rainbows after
The raindrops.

We Be Black, We've Been Blue

Everybody wants happiness, nobody wants pain.
But you can't have a rainbow without a little rain.

-Unknown

SELF-ESTEEM

SILENT TONES

PREFACE:
It's not what they see or say, but it's what you see and what you say about and to yourself. It's the enduring of those things no one knows and the overcoming of those things. It is the smile when you feel like crying. It's forgiving the unforgivable and the poise to walk away from those who don't appreciate and therefore don't deserve you. The beauty within speaks volumes, a good heart and right mind. The unique thing that makes you shine. The hidden yet empowering strengths that make you.

TONE:
Insightful

Silent tones, whispers unknown,
Words unspoken yet it shows
Inaudible to the ears, yet it's quite clear.
Deep rooted dwelling in the depths.
The innermost where quiet is kept.
Hard to conceal its great intensity,
Raging like a storming sea.
Filled with much complexity.
Hidden so the world can't see,
Elusive to the naked eye, greeted by a captivating smile.
Beauty beholds it,
Personality encamps it,
Disguised by a mask that hides its true identity.

Silent tones, whispers unknown words unspoken yet it shows.

We Be Black, We've Been Blue

Inaudible to the ears yet it's quite clear,
Listen with your heart,
Look into my eyes,
Look real closely. Better yet stare,
Stare into this window, into this soul of mine
Envision this sight that no one knows
Behold the innermost part of me.

I have with me purpose; I bathe and clothe myself in her. I look in the mirror and all I see is her.

-Rafequa C. Hall

SORRY NOT SORRY

PREFACE:
Don't change who you are to suit others.

TONE:
Empowerment

Sorry
I am not sorry.

I am
Brown sugar
But not as light as sugar cane
Broad nose
Coarse and coily hair
Four foot eleven
A gap between my teeth
A name too damn difficult
To speak…

I will not walk in this room
With my head held down.
I do not play chicken when I walk by
I am not afraid to look you in the eyes.
I am not uncomfortable
Being me.
I will not cower to bring you comfort
Compromising myself
To lessen your discomfort.
I will not change
I am not made

Rafequa C. Hall

To fit in
That's why I
Stand out.

I am not your
mainstream
Nor do I wish to be.

For those who deserted me
who hoped it would hurt me
I am
Still
Here
You didn't deserve me.

I will not dig beneath these
hills and hide
Toiling and mining your hate
Processing material
Worth less
Then dirt.

Your rejection once
Did
Hurt

But I had to learn.
My worth is more
Than gold
Refusing to give you
The power of making
Me bitter
I am better
Thank you

I am not who or
What you
Expect of me
Nor will I ever be.

I am
In competition
With no one
My greatest opponent
I am her and she is me,
Overcoming
Anxiety
Depression
And low self-esteem.
These blues be burdensome
A bit much to bear.
I've learned,
Faced my fears
I raise no white flags
Never giving up
Or giving in
I pull myself up
Out of the putrid pit of self-pity,
I fight with all determination.

To lose is not what I choose
I lift the weight
I felt the burn
I held it
I healed
I had to
I tough it through, some tough times too.
I've sung some weary blues changed

My tune.
I broke through barriers beautifully
Free
To
Be
Just who I am
As I am.
Even if
I stand alone
Out of the
Box is where
I'll be
Free
From
Your judgments…

I'll say it again

Sorry
I am not sorry.

I am not your
Mainstream
Nor do I wish
To be.

I am not
What you
Expect of me,
Nor will I ever be.

I am not
Your competition.

We Be Black, We've Been Blue

I am simply
Freely
Me.

Rafequa C. Hall

I don't live my life to please everybody because in doing so, you please nobody.

-Rafequa C. Hall

POETRY

&

SOLITUDE

PREFACE:
Poetry is defined as it is experienced. The release of all
things.

TONE:
Lighthearted

I am poetry and solitude.
This is what I love to do.
Uniquely uniting words
Joining adjectives with verbs.
Silently
I search
Intensely
Reminiscent
Triggering emotions and memories
Reciting while I'm writing.

It's medicine to my mind
It's therapy to my soul
Re-energizing

It's me, myself, and I
This is how I enjoy quality time
It's giving off peaceful vibes.

Rafequa C. Hall

I am
Poetry and solitude
A soothing breeze on a hot day
With a glass of lemonade.
Soothing as a scented candle,
Flickering in my darkly dimmed room
feeling the gentle flowing breeze.
Pleasantly passing by me.
Call me poetry and solitude.

I am
Free writing
Utilizing descriptive
Imagery and prose.
Loving how you read me aloud
Excuse me while I pause
Where the line drops.
Saying what I have to because I can.
Measure me in meters or not.

I let it flow and let it go where it goes.
Loving at the same time despising this
Invoking, empowering emotion of creative writing.

We Be Black, We've Been Blue

Poetry can tell us what human beings are. It can tell us why we stumble and fall and how, miraculously, we can stand up.

-Maya Angelou

RELATIONSHIPS

Rafequa C. Hall

DECEPTION IN YOUR EYES

PREFACE:
Resentment of a broken relationship.

TONE:
Hurt, Reflective, Resentment

Am I not as human as you?
Do I not have feelings too?
Hardened heart, resentful eyes,
Soul so full of bitter pride.
Although you see the tears in my eyes,
You continue to cast my feelings aside.
Still, I feed you with my last dime,
Offer my strength in your weakest times.
You continually take from me all my energy,
Leaving me lying listlessly.

Streams of blood run down my face,
My heart cries to see such pain from the one I love.
Whatever I do is never quite enough.
I could give my very life; I don't think you'd be satis-
fied.

You painted a picture that even the blind could see,
Except it wasn't transparent to me.
Cause I was in (what I thought was) love
Falling for this fallacy you called your reality.

We Be Black, We've Been Blue

Looks like I kissed the toad,
You know how the story goes.

Oh, silly me, what a fool I used to be
All for love I gave you all of me.

In return you set yourself free.

Funny though cause today I laugh, but yesterday I cried.

Oh, what a fool was I.
You know how they say
I wish I could turn back the hands of time.

Why wish? I'm reclaiming what's rightfully mine!

A peaceful mind,
Restful nights
No more swollen tearful eyes.

Treat me any kind of way
Thinking it's going to be okay.

Save that for another time,
Some other female cause I resign.

I write the script
You play the role
Cause this woman is in control!
Of her destiny
As far as I can see there is no future in you and me.

Once I have left the scene you'll soon regret.

Rafequa C. Hall

Realizing that all you have is time,
While you replay each moment of me in your mind.

Oh silly me what a fool I used to be,
All for love she gave her all for me.

Never allow someone to be your everything while allowing yourself to be just their option.

-Unknown

Rafequa C. Hall

HEARTBREAK

PREFACE:
When pain comes, we should learn from it and grow from it.

TONE:
Descriptive

Ooze, you deeply penetrated wound

Exude with puss, pain me if you must!
I welcome you to abound
Abound I pray
I beg you to stay
Lest I forget
The pain.

That though the heart is breaking, happiness can exist in a moment, also. And because the moment in which we live is all the time there really is, we can keep going.

- Zora Neale Hurston
Barracoon: The Story of the Last "Black Cargo"

ABUSE

Author's Insight:

Listen, love does not equal abuse.
When you are being abused, there is no denying it.
Your six senses - yes six, your intuition included -
will sound off alarms.

Stop believing the lies that:
- "he/she does this because they care for you."
- "It's my fault, I shouldn't have…"
- "Things will get better"
- "He/she meant well they just have to work on their anger"
- "Well, I'm partly to blame for the abuse be-cause…

There is no justification that will suffice.

Staying in a toxic relationship does not make you sub-missive, nor a good spouse or partner, and neither does it equate to unconditional love.

Enduring abuse is never ok. Abuse can be verbal, phys-ical, emotional, sexual, psychological in actions such as mental manipulation or intimidation.

Don't think for a second that it doesn't hurt anyone else because it affects everyone around you. It affects your kids, family and friends alike.

Value yourself enough to say enough is enough. Love yourself enough to walk away. Be real with yourself and call it what it is. Fight for you, in helping yourself you

will help to save someone else. Remember true love
starts first with you loving on you!

Love is patient and kind; love does not envy or boast; it is not arrogant or rude. It does not insist on its own way; it is not irritable or resentful; it does not rejoice at wrongdoing, but rejoices with the truth. Love bears all things, believes all things, hopes all things, endures all things. Love never ends.

-1 Corinthians 13:4–8a (ESV)

Rafequa C. Hall

TORN

PREFACE:
Fight for you

TONE:
Reflective, Frustration

He tears you apart tirelessly
You see it
You know it
You feel it
He disowns it.

Sis, might I remind you
Those hands of his
Wears rage like gloves.

He lacks empathy,
He lacks love

I patiently wait for the day
You say you're done.

He took power where none was given,
Where you were once strengthened
You became weakened.

His words,
A sledgehammer,
Used to beat your confidence into a

A shattered shame.

I know your heart had holes
You'd hope he'd heal.

Overstand that any hands
That find their way to hurt you
Surely can't heal too.

Your wounds be like
Uncontrolled vines
Wrapped up so tightly,
In and all around you.
Yet he finds the nerve to seductively
Whisper *I love you.*

Then he takes those same hands that
Hurt you
And explore you.

He dares
To take your confidence
And place it in a box of shame
He tells you to stand tall in it.

Restraining your words,
And emotional needs
To comfort his discomfort.

Sis,
His ego wears wounds like a tailored suit.
Taking his lack of confidence and placing it on you.

Suffocating in your emotions

Rafequa C. Hall

Stifled by your inability to express the stress he left
So you suppress the depression
Never lifting the weight he placed on your chest.

Queen,
Your cracked crown may be hard to conceal but
Build your broken confidence

This path you walk is paved
On a street with your name.
Hold your head up
And never ever be ashamed.

Your big beautiful eyes welled up with tears running
through
Like waterfalls
Rapidly rushing rivers of salt dangerously falling down
the cliffs of your eyes crashing beneath.

Beneath you,
Yes sis
This is
Beneath you,
You deserve better.

You need
To need you
More than you
Want him.

It's not the love of a man that makes your broken heart
whole.

Go without him

We Be Black, We've Been Blue

Go within you
Find peace to mend those broken pieces.

Truth is, though,
You are torn.
Tear yourself away
It may feel like pain
You have nothing to lose
Just self-love to gain.

The No. 1 reason women stay in abusive relation-
ships – because they're not able to take care of
themselves financially. It's also the No. 1 reason
why women go back.

- Kerry Washington

MORNING NEVER CAME

PREFACE:
Murder brought mourning and sorrow leaving no to-morrow.

TONE:
Sad

They say weeping may

Endure for a night

Her joy never came
In the morning light
Yet I'm still mourning her, because her morning
Never came
You took her life, and now ours will never be the
Same

Rafequa C. Hall

FIND HER

PREFACE:
Kids raised in domestically violent homes silently suffer
the effects of abuse.

TONE:
Trauma

I have too much pride
I'd rather hide my face from facing the mirror
So I don't have to face myself.

I try to beautify the lie
So I wear Maybelline.
I make believe
By painting a pretty picture
Laying it perfectly on my face
Hoping that no one will ever see

Hoping one day the pain will leave

But he stays

I can't stand to see the bruises

It tells stories of how he misuses me
I refuse to let him leave
You see

He has been my security

My insurance that covers my
Insecurities.

Needing a man to stay
Because I'm afraid of

Loneliness

Alone in this
I am
Alone

I am
A mother
Whose daughter has lost
Her only friend

Her eyes
A bright light beaming standing tall seeking frantically
Over a pitch-black night sea
Seeking
Desperately to find hope of a missing boat
Sadly, she would never
Find me
Missing right before her.

My daughter,
She lays in bed
She tells me her ears searches for signs of despair
Her heart races as she paces the floor
Waiting at the bedroom door.

She can hardly sleep
I taught her how to count sheep

Rafequa C. Hall

I even bought her the brightest night light.
I gave her a bible and tucked her in at night
Telling her everything will be alright

I cuddled then left her in a room of terror
To speak to Jesus, to tell him all about our troubles.
And not to tell no one else.
I taught her how to pray
Now I lay me down to sleep
I pray the lord my soul
To keep
If I should die before I wake
I pray the Lord my soul to take.
She hates it
I'm afraid she'll hate me

She's afraid to leave me
Shadows of fear taunt her ten-year-old mind.
The sounds of my cries
Crippled her over the years
A victim, her and I.

I told her a child should be seen
Not heard and now she

Never speaks.

I search for her
Through her eyes
I look for her with all my might.

A bright light beaming standing tall seeking frantically
Over a pitch-black night sea.
Seeking,

Desperately to find hope
Of a missing boat.
Sadly, I can't
Find her.
Missing right before me

My daughter

Family is supposed to be our safe haven. Very often it is the place where we find the deepest heartache.

- Iyanla Vanzant

BREAKING HER SILENCE

PREFACE:
Abusive relationship that led to a tragic end.

TONE:
Trauma, Abuse

Her mother
Boasted:
Baby, you've been blessed from birth.

Brave and bold she was told to be.

Be brilliant,
Become the very best,
Be all… that you can be!

Brown skin tone,
Breathtakingly
Beautiful
Black young lady, she was strong and bold
Beaming with life, she had bright eyes with a
Bubbly personality
Barely 20 she

Began to date this
Brotha, he was
Bodied down with

Big
Bulging
Biceps.

Blinded by what she thought was love, she was
Bamboozled by this fool

Believe me, baby
Baby, you belong to me.
Baby, I'm gonna make you my world.
Baby, you're gonna be my wife.
Baby, I'm gonna give you the finer things in life.
Before she knew it, she was swooned so smoothly
By his softly stated lies.
Before she knew it, her dream guy pranced around with
a disguise.

Blacklisted from her family and friends.
Breaking her spirit and
Bashing her confidence
Banning her from a life she once knew.

Baffled she became, as he transformed, warped into this
Belligerent, bloodthirsty bum.
Belittling her by replacing her name with BITCH!
Bent on arguing absentees, making absolutely astonish-
ing accusations
Brazen
Barefaced
Bitter, he was a
Bantering Brute, we all hated him for what we knew
he'd do.

Blow for blow.
Black and blue.
Body badly beaten... and
Bruised.
Brave it! Is what she thought she'd do.
By staying, she committed, he loves me, we'll make it
through.

But he was abusive, and she'd never admit it
Believing it would get better
Backslaps
Backstabs as she nursed
Broken legs
Broken arms
Broken ribs
Broken heart
Begging yet hanging on
But his behavior got worse as he began to stalk her.
Cheating is what he
Believed

Boiling like a kettle shooting spouts of steam,
Boom, bullets blasting from the barrel, while she re-
leases
Blood-curdling screams
Boom bullets pierced her tiny fragile body, she fell to
the ground
Blanketed in her warm blood, she lay dying
Boom, another
Blasting bullet blazing from the barrel
Bastard took his life

Bursting into the room
Before her mother's eyes

Barely alive, her mother held her
Baby close to her
Bosom with all her might
Begging her baby not to leave
Begging to God *please don't let this be*

But now…these
Broken spirits will
Break no more
By
Breaking their silence
Beyond the grave
By
Bellowing the stories of the abused now
buried. No one listens to silent cries
Beyond the four walls. Nevertheless, untold stories
Beyond the grave
By sharing their stories

I hope to save
Save someone from ending up the same way
And convince the abused
Not to stay

The pain they covered up
With their smiles
I miss them, all the time
In memory of my two girlfriends
I wish this wasn't the
End
End
Domestic violence
Prevent the
Next story from

Ending like this
REST IN ETERNAL PEACE

Rafequa C. Hall

In an abusive relationship – we'll talk about men and women – women are often restrained, by words or out of fear, from leaving. They will tolerate abuse up to and including being put to death.

-Rene Marie

AFFIRMATIONS

Be kind to yourself by speaking life over yourself. Be aware of your thoughts, they are seeds put to the soil and will produce what is sown.

- I am worthy of Love.
- I am not a victim, I am victorious.
- I am stronger every day.
- I am grateful.
- I am powerful.
- I am loved.
- I am abundant.
- I am blessed.
- I am a child of God.
- I am open to receiving.
- I believe in myself.
- I am confident.
- I am fearless.
- I am powerful.
- I am beautiful.
- I accept myself.
- I am a great person.
- My feelings are valid.
- I refuse to give up or give in.
- I give myself grace to face each new day.
- Every day I am stronger, wiser and better.
- I will not give up on me.
- I will fight for me.
- I will not lose, I will win.
- I am encouraged, I am courageous, I will not be defeated.
- God grants me grace to face each day.

- I can do all things through God who strengthens me.
- I am perfect being me.
- I am enough.
- I am a winner.
- I am capable.
- I am worthy.
- I am healed.
- I am divinely guided in all that I do.
- I am honorable.
- I can overcome the hardships in my life.
- I walk by faith and not by sight.
- Fear has no power over me.
- No weapon formed against me shall prosper and every tongue that rises up against me shall be condemned.
- I am not a failure, and it is ok to make mistakes.
- I am greater than I believe.
- I am noble, brave and strong.

RESOURCES
& FACTS

Abuse
- NATIONAL DOMESTIC VIOLENCE 2/7 HOTLINE Call: 1(800) 799- SAFE (7233)
- Send text to sms:88788
- Website: https://www.thehotline.org/

Common Signs of Abusive Nature in Relationships:
- Telling you that you never do anything right.
- Showing extreme jealousy of your friends or time spent away from them.
- Preventing or discouraging you from spending time with friends, family members, or peers.
- Insulting, demeaning, or shaming you, especially in front of other people.
- Preventing you from making your own decisions, including about working or attending school.
- Controlling finances in the household without discussion, including taking your money or refusing to provide money for necessary expenses.
- Pressuring you to have sex or perform sexual acts you're not comfortable with.
- Pressuring you to use drugs or alcohol.
- Intimidating you through threatening looks or actions.
- Insulting your parenting or threatening to harm or take away your children or pets.
- Intimidating you with weapons like guns, knives, bats, or mace.

- Destroying your belongings or your home.
- https://www.thehotline.org/identify-abuse/domestic-abuse-warning-signs/

ANXIETY
SCRIPTURES

At a time when you need mental healing these scriptures are here to remedy you back to a healthy "state of mind."

Psalm 91:2
- Search me, O God, and know my heart; test me and know my anxious thoughts.

Psalm 37:5
- Commit everything you do to the Lord. Trust him, and he will help you.

2 Timothy 1:7
- For God has not given us a spirit of fear and timidity but of power, love, and self-discipline.

Matthew 6:25
- That is why I tell you not to worry about everyday life—whether you have enough food and drink, or enough clothes to wear. Isn't life more than food, and your body more than clothing?

Matthew 6:34
- So don't worry about tomorrow, for tomorrow will bring its own worries. Today's trouble is enough for today.

Matthew 11:28
- Then Jesus said, "Come to me, all of you who are weary and carry heavy burdens, and I will give you rest.

Luke 12:25-26
- Can all your worries add a single moment to your life? And if worry can't accomplish a little thing like that, what's the use of worrying over bigger things?

Thessalonians 3:16

- Now may the Lord of peace himself give you his peace at all times and in every situation. The Lord be with you all.

John 14:27

- I am leaving you with a gift—peace of mind and heart. And the peace I give is a gift the world cannot give. So don't be troubled or afraid.

1 John 4:18

- Such love has no fear because perfect love expels all fear. If we are afraid, it is for fear of punishment, and this shows that we have not fully experienced his perfect love.

CITATIONS

SURE, MUST BE SOMETHING

- https://en.wikipedia.org/wiki/African_empires
- https://www.historydefined.net/the-most-pow-erful-kings-in-african-history/
- https://kidadl.com/baby-names/inspira-tion/african-queen-names-from-the-past-present-mythology

HARMONY NEVER HAD A HOME

- http://www.myblackhistory.net/Jim_crow.htm

WE BE BLACK WE'VE BEEN BLUE

- https://en.wikipedia.org/wiki/Tulsa_race_mas-sacre#Aftermath
- http://www.blackwallstreet.freeserv-ers.com/The%20Story.htm
- https://www.nytimes.com/interac-tive/2021/05/24/us/tulsa-race-massacre.html

Quotation Citations

"WHAT HAPPENS WHEN THE NEXT GENERA-TION SEARCHES NOT FOR THE TRUTH AND SETTLES TO DRINK FROM THE BITTER FOUN-TAIN OF RACE COMPLACENCY?"

-RAFEQUA C. HALL

"A people without the knowledge of their history, origin and culture is like a tree without roots."

- Marcus Garvey

"It is that which constitutes our real and best nour- ish-ment. What we are merely taught seldom nourishes the mind like that which we teach our- selves."

-Carter G. Woodson
The Mis-Education of The Negro

"Music is an expression of harmony in sound. Love is an expression of harmony in life."

- Stephen Gaskins

"It takes black keys and white keys to make perfect Har-mony."

-Benny Goodman

"There is but one coward on earth, and that is the cow-ard that dare not know."

- W.E.B. DuBois
Dusk of Dawn

"The tragedy of life is not found in failure but com-placency. Not in you doing too much, but doing too lit-tle. Not in you living above your means, but be- low your capacity. It's not failure but aiming too low, that is life's greatest tragedy."

- Benjamin E. Mays

"We are our own healing place."

- Melvina Young

"She is a friend of mine. She gathers me, man. The pieces I am, she gathers them and gives them back to me in all the right order."

- Toni Morrison

"Abandon the cultural myth that all female friend- ships must be bitchy, toxic or competitive. This myth is like heels and purses- pretty but designed to slow women down."

- Roxane Gay

"A friend is one who knows us, but loves us anyway."
- Jerome Cummings

Si-sta: noun
The best kind of friend

"Sistamotherfriend: A friend that is more than a friend."
- Rafequa C. Hall

"I love to think of nature as an unlimited broadcast- ing station, through which God speaks to us every hour, if we will only tune in."

- George Washington Carver

"You may not control all the events that happen to you, but you can decide not to be reduced by them."

- Maya Angelou

"The country is in deep trouble. We've forgotten that a rich life consists fundamentally of serving others, trying to leave the world a little better than you found it. We need the courage to question the powers that be, the courage to be impatient with evil and pa- tient with people, the courage to fight for social justice. In many instances we will be stepping out on nothing, and just hoping to land on something. But that's the struggle. To live is to wrestle with despair, yet never allow despair to have the last word."

- Cornel West

"Never forget that justice is what love looks like in public."

- Cornel West

"Everybody wants happiness, nobody wants pain. But you can't have a rainbow without a little rain."

- Unknown

"I have with me purpose; I bathe and clothe myself in her. I look in the mirror and all I see is her."

- Rafequa C. Hall

"I don't live my life to please everybody because in doing so, you please nobody."

- Rafequa C. Hall

"Poetry can tell us what human beings are. It can tell us why we stumble and fall and how, miraculously, we can stand up."

- Maya Angelou

"Never allow someone to be your everything while allowing yourself to be just their option."

- Unknown

"That though the heart is breaking, happiness can exist in a moment, also. And because the moment in which we live is all the time there really is, we can keep going."

- Zora Neale Hurston
Barracoon: The Story of the Last "Black Cargo"

"The No. 1 reason women stay in abusive relation- ships – because they're not able to take care of themselves financially. It's also the No. 1 reason why women go back."

- Kerry Washington

"Family is supposed to be our safe haven. Very often it is the place where we find the deepest heartache."

- Iyanla Vanzant

"In an abusive relationship – we'll talk about men and women – women are often restrained, by words or out of fear, from leaving. They will tolerate abuse up to and including being put to death"

-Rene Marie

SPECIAL ACKNOWLEDGMENTS

Finding time to write did not come easy; it was a sacrifice of a lot of things. It was a necessary road to take.

I always say God is forever faithful, because he truly is consistent through every season. Instead of losing myself in the most traumatic times, Father, you took me and taught me how to stitch the torn pieces of my life. You taught me how to smile while dealing with pain and brought me unspeakable peace while resting in the midst of a raging sea. You showed me where to find my joy when it was misplaced, and you continue to send me goldfinches on my rainiest days.

I am truly inspired by our resilience, black beauty, and black power. I am forever grateful to our legacy holders of yesterday, our ancestors whose past paved our way. They lead with greatness and integrity. Our history is so empowering and uplifting. I love us. I'm just saying we are all that and then some. Never ever forget where we came from as a people.

To my husband, I thank you for having my back when I had to shut everything down during this process. You were so patient with me in the moments where I needed to be silent and shut down to go within. With our lives so busy, it's hard to make moments like that happen, but you were so selfless and supportive throughout. You doubted me not for a second, always offering moments of praise, pushing me to finish strong, and that I did! Love you Junie B.

To our kids, Ains, Lannie, and Lyssie, you make every day so darn meaningful! You're the best part of your dad and I; you make life so worth living. You make my "want to" so intense and it keeps me driven. When your dad and I do what we do, it is done intentionally. It is to teach you and expect you to do life better than we did! Thank you for lending your listening ears to hear me recite poetry randomly without end at the top of my lungs, lol. Love you three. Alanna thank you for gracing my book with your illustrations.

This book was based on the perspective of life as a black woman. My greatest example of that is my mother. As a child, I would put on my mother's shoes, clothes, and perfume. I did this thinking it would make me feel closer to her. Mom, thank you for being a great example, and thank you for sacrificing so much. Thank you for never giving up.

Thank you to Amanda Chambers of Divine Legacy Publishing and team.

Symone Miller, author of *The Life of Legacy Lear Green*, thank you.

My sister Althea Willis, author of *Saving Karmen,* you took this leap of faith. You did it and now I've finally finished. Xox

My sistermotherfriend who always feels my pain, cheers me on, cried at the reading of my poems just because you were proud. Love you, you bring the best of me out.

Lashanda Manning, thank you for your support and lifelong friendship.

Thank you to Tavia and Roy for your positive words and encouragement.

ACKNOWLEDGMENTS

My Dad: Clive

Step-parents: BJ & Lavern

Siblings: Zulehka, Cherene, Makeda, Thea, Shamelil, Khalil, Kirk

Step Siblings: Flo, Joe, Tee Tee, Avis, Lionel, Renita, Angie, Julianna, Holly, Corey, RIP Kenny

Nieces & Nephews: Chey, Lilac, Jada, Jaylen, Cici, CJ

In-laws: Kav, Cav, Wave, Ash, Joe, Winst, Heather, April, Lamar, Wes. RIP Mums.

Close friends, my aunts and uncles, cousins. Too many to list, thank you much love and blessings XOOX

CONNECT
WITH THE AUTHOR

Website: www.rafequathewriter.com

Facebook: Rafequa Hall

Instagram: @rafequathewriter

Divine Legacy
PUBLISHING, LLC.

Creative Control With Self-Publishing

Divine Legacy Publishing provides authors with the guid-ance necessary to take creative control of their work through self-publishing. We provide:

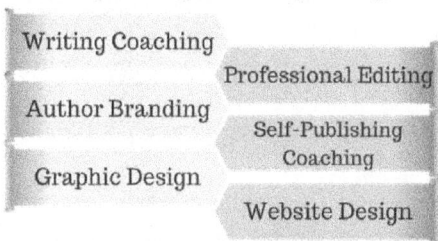

Writing Coaching

Professional Editing

Author Branding

Self-Publishing Coaching

Graphic Design

Website Design

Let Divine Legacy Publishing help you master the business of self-publishing.

www.ingramcontent.com/pod-product-compliance
Lightning Source LLC
Chambersburg PA
CBHW071857020426
42331CB00010B/2553